Tigers

Leo Statts

abdopublishing.com

Published by Abdo Zoom™, PO Box 398166, Minneapolis, Minnesota 55439. Copyright © 2017 by Abdo Consulting Group, Inc. International copyrights reserved in all countries. No part of this book may be reproduced in any form without written permission from the publisher. Abdo Zoom™ is a trademark and logo of Abdo Consulting Group, Inc.

Printed in the United States of America, North Mankato, Minnesota
062016
092016

**THIS BOOK CONTAINS
RECYCLED MATERIALS**

Cover Photo: Shutterstock Images
Interior Photos: Potapov Alexander/Shutterstock Images, 1; iStockphoto, 4, 5, 15; Shutterstock Images, 6, 12, 13; Dirk Freder/iStockphoto, 7, 18; Sergey Uryadnikov/Shutterstock Images, 8–9; Nachiketa Bajaj/Shutterstock Images, 9; Gregg Brekke/Shutterstock Images, 10–11; Red Line Editorial, 11, 20 (left), 20 (right), 21 (left), 21 (right); Amit Rane/iStockphoto, 14–15; Mark Malkinson Photography/iStockphoto, 16; Sarah Cheriton-Jones/iStockphoto, 17

Editor: Emily Temple
Series Designer: Madeline Berger
Art Direction: Dorothy Toth

Publisher's Cataloging-in-Publication Data
Names: Statts, Leo, author.
Title: Tigers / by Leo Statts.
Description: Minneapolis, MN : Abdo Zoom, [2017] | Series: Savanna animals |
    Includes bibliographical references and index.
Identifiers: LCCN 2016941160 | ISBN 9781680792034 (lib. bdg.) |
    ISBN 9781680793710 (ebook) | ISBN 9781680794601 (Read-to-me ebook)
Subjects: LCSH: Tigers--Juvenile literature.
Classification: DDC 599.756--dc23
LC record available at http://lccn.loc.gov/2016941160

Table of Contents

Tigers

Tigers are the biggest members of the cat family.

Their roars are loud.
They can be heard far away.

Tigers are good swimmers.

They can swim several
miles at a time.

Body

Tigers have thick fur.
It is reddish with dark stripes.

A tiger's stripes are like fingerprints.
Every tiger has a different pattern.

Habitat

Tigers live in Asia.
Bengal tigers are
most common.
They live in India.

Where tigers live

Tigers live in **savannas**.

They are also found in
rain forests and swamps.

Food

Tigers hunt alone.
They eat meat. Deer and antelope are common food.
They also eat water buffalo.

Tigers have two or three babies.
The babies are called cubs.

They stay with their mothers for two years.

Tigers spend most of their lives alone. They live for 10 to 15 years.

Average Length

A tiger is as long as a sofa.

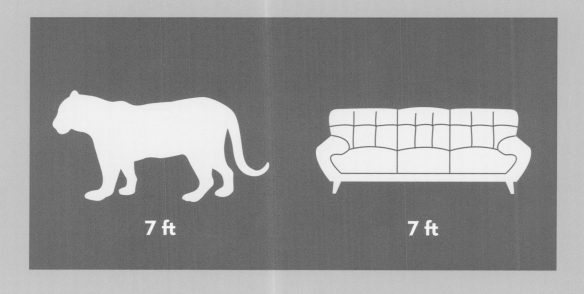

7 ft   7 ft

Average Weight

A tiger weighs less than a baby grand piano.

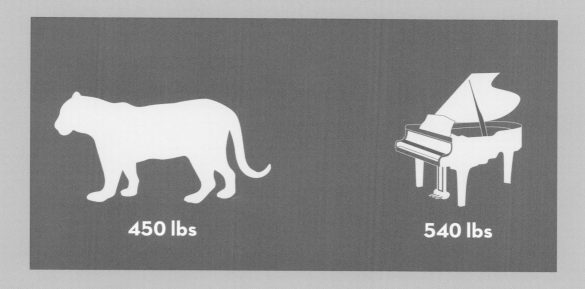

450 lbs   540 lbs

Glossary

cub - a young animal.

pattern - a regular marking.

rain forest - a tropical woodland where it rains a lot.

savanna - a grassland with few or no trees.

swamp - wet land that is filled with trees, plants, or both.

Booklinks

For more information
on tigers, please visit
booklinks.abdopublishing.com

Z**m In on Animals!

Learn even more with the Abdo Zoom
Animals database. Check out
abdozoom.com for more information.

Index